Have you ever gone fishing? How was it? What did you use? Were you in a boat?

Fishing Boats!
Different Types of Fishing Boats From Bass Boats to Walk-arounds
(Boats for Kids)
Children's Boats & Ships Books

Left Brain Kids
Educational Books for Children

A fishing vessel is a boat or a ship. It is mainly used to catch fish in the sea or on a lake or river. Both large and small fishing vessels play their part, for getting food or having fun. Get to know some of them on the next pages!

Bass boats!

These are small fishing boats. People use this kind of boat in freshwater fishing such as on lakes, rivers and streams.

Modern bass boats have swivel chairs which allow the angler to fish in any direction. They are equipped with fishing tackle and equipment like lures and rods.

Bay boats!

These boats are used for simple coastal saltwater fishing.

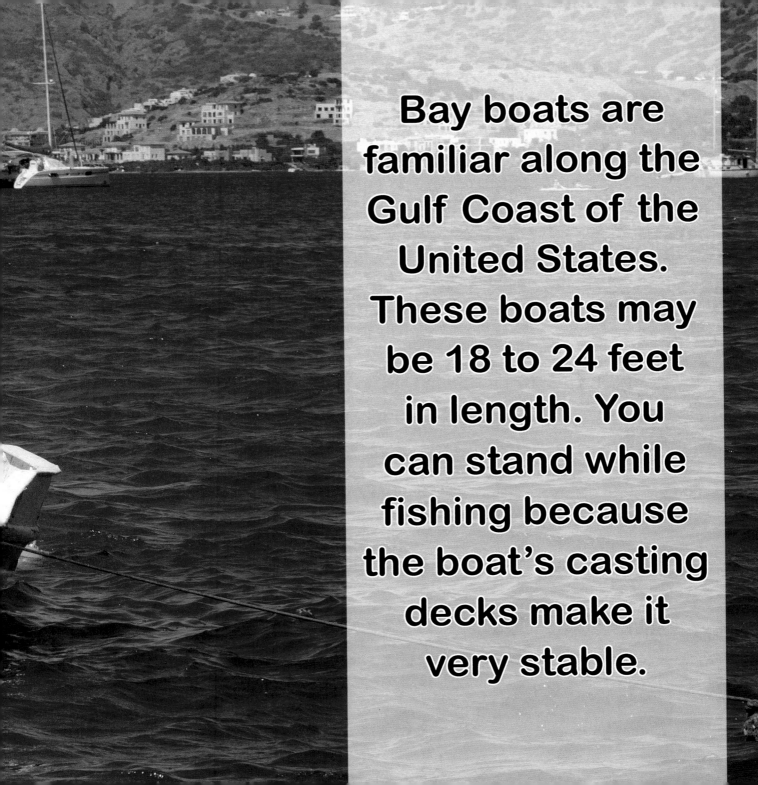

Bay boats are familiar along the Gulf Coast of the United States. These boats may be 18 to 24 feet in length. You can stand while fishing because the boat's casting decks make it very stable.

Sport-fishing boats!

These are bigger fishing boats.

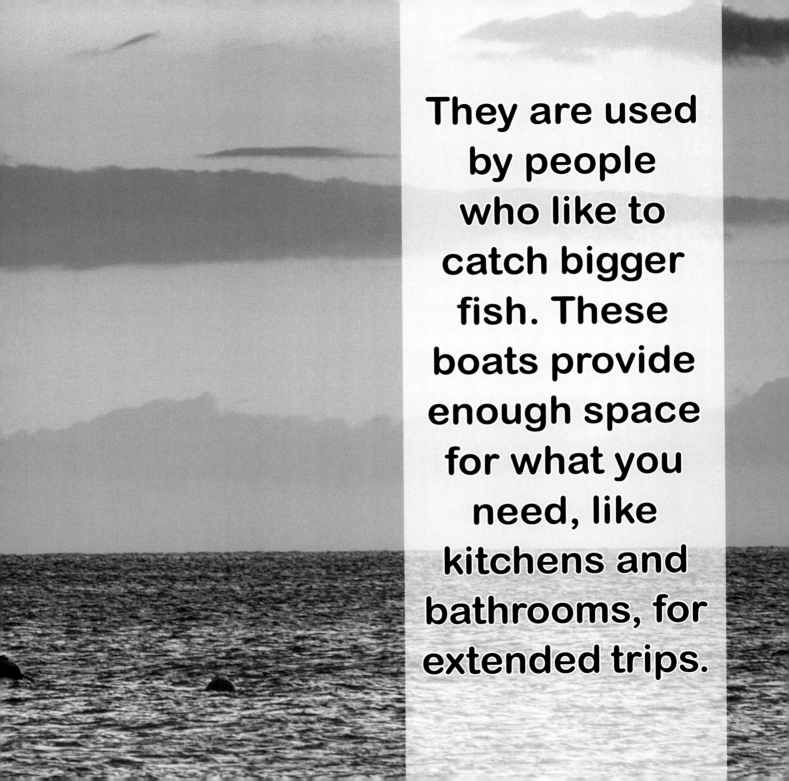

They are used by people who like to catch bigger fish. These boats provide enough space for what you need, like kitchens and bathrooms, for extended trips.

Jon Boats!

These are flat-bottomed boats with one to three bench seats.

These simple boats fit sport fishing and hunting. Their hulls are nearly flat, which lets the boat ride over the waves. But Jon boats can get in trouble on windy days or in rough water. These boats are simple and easy to maintain.

Seiners!

These vessels are used for ocean fishing.

They are named after the seine fishing nets they use. The nets are designed to haul fish found near the water's surface. The seiner is equipped with state-of-the-art navigation and fish-finding equipment to ensure a good catch!

Longliners!

These fishing vessels employ long fishing lines with around 1,000 lures on each. From the boat's tail end, the fishing line is deployed.

Using its automated systems, the longliner stays in place and reels in the fish to be stored.

Kayak!

This is a means of transportation for one or two people.

It is also a quiet way of approaching wary fish. Due to its environmentally friendly appeal, kayak fishing has gained popularity in recent times.

Pontoon!

This boat is like a floating room. It depends on two or more pontoons to float.

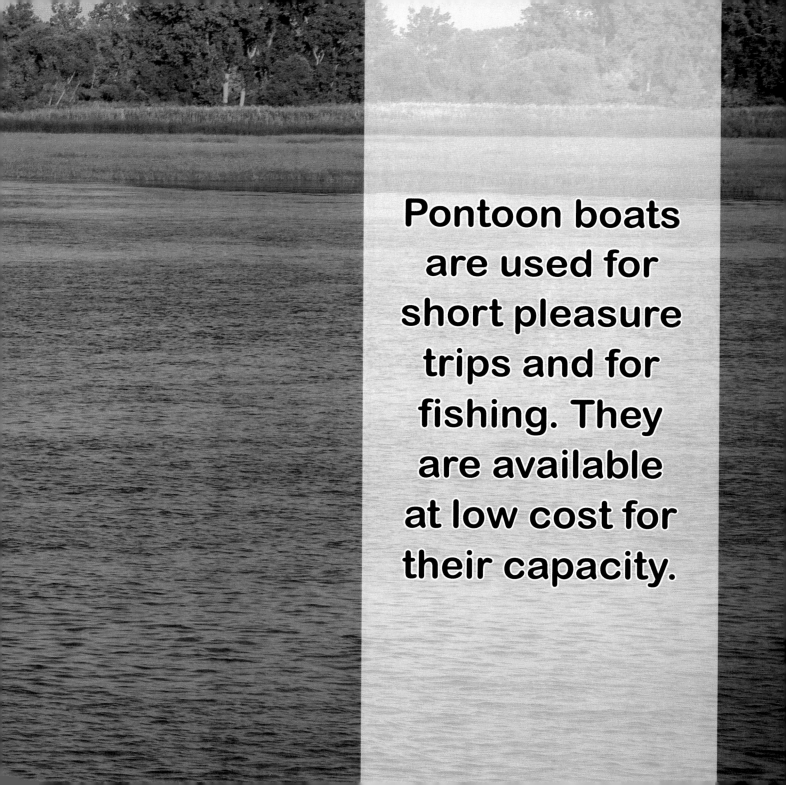

Pontoon boats are used for short pleasure trips and for fishing. They are available at low cost for their capacity.

Are you hooked on fishing? Maybe you want to experience this exciting activity with your family and friends. Now you know more about which boat you should choose!

Made in the USA
Middletown, DE
07 July 2021